TABLE OF CONTENTS

Seven Confessions of an Old Furniture Marketer

By

Willie Davis

I forgot I had these 842 furniture phrases. I almost recycle binned these from my computer's hard drive. 17 years of collecting some great words would have gone bye-bye!

Sorry!

Whew!

Background…I was a marketing consultant in the home furnishings industry for 19 years – working with small to medium size independent furniture retailers. I set ad budgets, developed ad plans, and then implemented them. My radio, TV, direct mail, and print advertising campaigns drew the traffic that bought their furniture.

I'm no longer in the furniture industry, not really. A little marketing help here and there for retailers who ask for it, but that's about it.

The home furnishings industry was good to me. Even with 19 years experience, I was a young whipper-snapper veteran compared to the thousands of furniture veterans doing daily battle in the industry. Still, 19 years was long enough to develop some deep-seated perceptions that I'm now willing to confess in writing.

They say that confessions are good for the soul…so, here goes!

First confession…I love the furniture industry.

Second confession…I hate the furniture industry.

…First, the love…

…humans need furniture to live. Something to sit on. Eat on. Sleep on. I marveled at Market, whether in North Carolina, Tupelo, or Vegas, how an industry can design and manufacture such beautiful furniture. The woods. The fabrics. The leathers. The creativeness. The craftsmanship. The passion.

I was always fascinated how all the pieces and people found each other to make something so functional, so attractive, and so available to the masses?

…And second, the hate…

…how could an industry with such a public need, and the skill to fill that need, choose to sell that need like a prostitute on the street corner?

The industry loves its scream and shout its promotions. Yes, I agree, there is a time for promotional advertising…but not all the time?

I encouraged my clients to get off the street corner, but, it didn't work. I eventually succumbed to the songs of the Sirens and became well skilled in the art of *'Ends Monday at 8'* advertising. I learned how to draw a crowd with my eyes closed.

"Four days only. Wall to wall sale. You don't pay a dime until you want to. While they last. Closed today to get ready for tomorrow. Sure it's a private sale. You didn't bring that invitation in? OK, no problem! Lowest prices of the season. Lowest prices of the year. Lowest prices ever. Can we let that floor model go? Sure, why not? Did I mention that you pay or don't pay a bunch of NOs?"

The client requests I kept hearing… *"Willie, I just need some more traffic. Willie, you bring them in and I'll sell them. Willie, that was great! What's next? Willie, how soon can we run that again?"*

I loved this one. *"Willie, your advertising didn't work this weekend. 160 people came in but nobody bought anything."* I fired that client.

I once ran a successful Millard Fillmore Birthday Sale for a small Pennsylvania store that had been circling the drain for years. Only a miniscule number of Americans know that Millard was our 13th President, and less have a clue when he was born. Didn't matter. It was a two-for-the-price-of-one, free springs, and the store owner was not hiding the good stuff weekend. I celebrated Millard's birthday two times that year in two separate markets.

I learned that combining the right amount of print with the right amount of radio with the right voice at the right time was like throwing a match in a pool of gasoline – traffic exploded! I learned how to stretch a client's advertising dollars and how to select the right media. I even learned how to fire long-standing media with grace. However, I think the ABC affiliate in Toledo might still have a price on my head for taking them out of the advertising mix. That rep lost thousands of commission dollars.

I learned the ins and outs of advertising poker in a market. I learned when to play and when to go get beer and chips with my client's ad dollars. I learned to count success…not by the weekend traffic but by the number of advertising poker hands I won in a year for my client.

And, most importantly, I learned to identify quickly when a potential client had a marketing problem, a competitor problem, or an organizational problem. I learned that increasing traffic only hastened the demise of a poorly run store.

Third confession…I am appreciative of my clients and the people I worked with for those 19 years because I was able to learn so much about marketing.

If that really sounds self-serving…well, it is. Marketers don't readily admit the inside secret of how they develop deep smarts on their client's money.

While honing my scream and shout promotional skills…I read hundreds of marketing books. I attended multiple seminars yearly. I fiddled with more seductive copywriting and different ways of telling different creation stories.

I began to answer questions in the home furnishings industry that nobody was asking.

I learned that there is one word that explains why Mr. Jones (our mythical persona) reaches into her pocketbook and gives a retailer her money. Yep, one word. I defined that word mathematically. I took that one word math formula and developed other math formulas to better describe how traffic is built, sales are won, and market share is gained.

I learned to teach this math lesson on a napkin to those who would listen.

I started rereading poetry to better understand writing rhythm. I reread some of the great fiction authors to better understand how they paint mental images. How their words take you places in your mind. I'm still floored at those last few pages of Steinbeck's *Grapes of Wrath.*

I studied the brain. How do our senses accept external communications? How are words and visual images transformed to provide meaning, or dumped in the 'I don't care' word bin? How does a series of communications get past Broca, through the pre-frontal cortex and branded into the right brain's long term memory?

I started writing some Peterman product copy. Nope, didn't find any real industry interest here in this writing style. It is always easier to say, "Was $1,200…Now $999."

Item Name: Green Cabinet with Screen Door
Description: What do you do with an old East Texas home when it's torn down? Well, you certainly don't throw it away, not with decades of love aged into the wood. Take that screen door, you know, the door that always knew where you were going – and where you had been! Surround it with some ceiling and old cabinet boards. Leave the screw nail holes. They're cool. Tie it all together with some smile memories (I suggest you leave out that night on Highway 101). What you now stand in front of is a portal to your past, a touch of home. No, it wasn't your home, but it could have been. 30" wide, 17" deep, 80" high. Three shelves to hold your new memories. Sure, life now can be lived without this cabinet, but not as well. $999 for a walk down memory lane.

Item Name: King Hickory Bustle Back All Leather Chair and Ottoman
Description: Dark Hunter Green. All leather. It's not the chair. It's the air of romance that surrounds it. Those who sit in it have closer attention paid to them. People listen more carefully to what is said and who is saying it. There's an added dash to posture. It's not merely a chair. It's the high ground in the room. Why settle for someplace to sit when there's a place you can prolong your winning streak.

I wrote a weekly Crash Course in Marketing that was e-mailed out to clients. Did this for over 200 weeks. A couple of hundred words each Tuesday morning. Mostly on marketing topics that interested me at that time. No Hemingway awards here, but each crash always made some point I hoped clients would ponder.

And finally, to your benefit now, I started collecting furniture words and phrases that could educate and persuade potential customers. A promotion that works in Des Moines, IA could also work in Harrisburg, PA. My Willie, 'don't reinvent the wheel' concept.

When I wrote a phrase I liked in radio copy or a print ad I would jot it down. When I saw a phrase in a trade magazine I would jot it down. When I was driving home and thought of an interesting word combination I would jot it down. I think I paid someone to write me some jot downs in a particular category one time. Don't remember who or when.

Somehow, I have jotted down 842 phrases over those furniture years. These 842 jot downs have been sitting on my hard drive gathering dust since 2009. Forgot all about them. Ran across them a few weeks ago while cleaning out some computer files.

Actually, there are more than 842 here. I started using some of these as templates. Pick one and see if you can modify it to fit another category. I used the…'can hold eight kids, four hound dogs and a piggy you stole from the shed' line multiple ways and times.

I did get into trouble once when I let approved a radio spot to run deep in the heart of Baptist country. It shouted that the sale was, *"hotter than Aunt Ida's undies."* I did you a favor and deleted that phrase from the list. You don't have to search for it.

These 842 phrases are yours now. You can have them. Do the public a favor and make some good use out of them.

Fourth confession…I met a lot of wonderful people in the home furnishing industry. Loved them. They have a heart for the industry and the work they do. They get it.

Also, I met a lot of people who are working in the industry because there is no other industry they can work in. Job city. Lipstick on the pig thing. Living in the Graveyard of Bad Intentions. But, as I have aged, I've learned that these folks are in every industry. Get over it Willie. I have.

Fifth confession…I hate the industry's UP system. No, despise is a more politically correct term.

Who invented this puppy? 100 people walk into a furniture store. 75 walk out with nothing but a negative perception. Will someone step forward and implement something that works? The industry should be closing at above 50%.

The industry can do better, but what do I know?

Sixth confession...I wish I could have moved more people off the 'all the time' promotional dime and onto the 'some times' seduction train.

Transactional advertising has always ruled over relationship advertising in the home furnishings industry. Early in my career I was naïve enough to believe it was one or the other. I now know that the answer is a combination of seduction and promotion. The challenge is to stay within the budget, get the right message with the right media, and have the patience for the seduction seed to harvest.

Seventh (and last) confession (here)... For all practical purposes, the furniture industry is in my rear-view mirror. I have mixed emotions about that.

Before the home furnishings industry I had 14 years in the criminal justice system – teaching at the Ohio State Reformatory before it became the famous Shawshank movie prison. I have returned to the criminal justice system and thrown my heart into helping offenders prosocially reintegrate into society.

A lot of the work I am doing now is the result of what I have learned in the furniture industry. The industry will be indirectly helping society reduce crime. The industry will never know. Go figure.

I will forever be appreciative of that.

Willie

PS: I can be reached at willied@neo.rr.com

Furniture Phraseology

GENERAL

<u>*Headings*</u>

1. Furnishing your home from kitchen to home office has never been more fun
2. Furnishing your home from kitchen to home office has never been easier
3. We have your total package in home furnishing
4. Total value and total selection in home furnishings
5. You'll love the new looks we can bring to your home
6. Brighten up your home with a new look today
7. The best furniture at the best prices
8. Look no more for great deals on great furniture
9. Everything you need for every room in the house
10. Renovate your home without lifting a hammer - our beautiful furniture will transform any room
11. Choose the style, the color and the brand - and put together a great new look
12. Transform your home with beautiful new furnishings
13. Complete home furnishings that make any home more beautiful
14. Complete home furnishings to make your home more beautiful
15. Bright ideas to brighten your home

<u>*Introductory Statements*</u>

1. Make your home more comfortable, more beautiful and more enjoyable with furniture and accessories for every room.
2. You want furniture that does more than just look good. You want it to look good, feel good and be good…all at a good price. You've come to the right place.
3. Inspired by the beauty of furniture fashioned by early colonial craftsmen, which means you'll rest in the classic warmth and gracefulness of our nation's past.

SAVINGS

Headings

1. Competitive prices every day
2. Our buying group = your savings
3. Save every day at _____
4. Great furniture, great prices
5. Best prices you'll find
6. Prices that fit your budget
7. Prices that make you smile
8. You'll love these buys
9. Save more at _____
10. Generous savings plus free financing bring your dreams to reality
11. Low on money? You can still get terrific quality furniture
12. See how far your money can go
13. We can help you s-t-r-e-t-c-h your furniture dollars
14. Savor the savings
15. Join the crowd! Our volume discounts save everyone money
16. Furniture that fits every budget
17. Keep more money in your wallet
18. Keep more money in your wallet with these tremendous savings
19. Save your sanity and your money – you'll find the best buys in town right here
20. Save your time and your money – you'll find the best buys in town right here
21. Enjoy great furniture and great savings at the same time

SELECTION

Headings

1. Choices, choices, choices
2. All your favorite brand names
3. All the best brands
4. Choose from the best
5. Pick your favorites
6. Terrific selection of sofas
7. The best choices for your home
8. Choose your own style
9. Imagine It . . . Find It
10. Tremendous selections and tremendous buys for your entire home

KNOWLEDGEABLE STAFF

Headings

1. A staff that cares
2. We know furniture
3. We inform. You decide
4. Dedicated to meeting your needs
5. Our staff cares
6. Our staff knows furniture
7. Our staff helps you choose
8. We treat you right
9. Meet our friendly staff
10. Enjoy our friendly staff
11. Our staff puts you first
12. We want to earn your trust through service
13. Browse or buy

DINING ROOMS

Headings

1. Dining rooms that say, 'Pull up a chair!'
2. Good food, good conversation, great seating
3. Dining furniture that showcases what you dish up…and handles what your family dishes out
4. Good looking and tough…dinettes that work
5. Undeniable beauty - our solid oak dining collection
6. And undeniable value - solid oak. With less you get more! Solid wood dining room savings
7. Save money without sacrificing style
8. Serving up savings on solid wood dining furniture
9. Serving up savings on solid wood dinettes
10. The smiles…the food…the special memories
11. Serve your best on the best … (brand name) dining rooms
12. Memorable holiday meals reflected in the beauty of wood. Dining rooms by (brand name)
13. Delicate china…polished silver…burnished oak
14. Gather the family around the table
15. Dining rooms that make the meal
16. Great furniture for great meals
17. The dining room - the place your family gathers
18. Dining rooms that draw family and friends together
19. Great dining rooms at great prices
20. Elegant dining in the comfort of your home

21. Sturdy and beautiful dining sets
22. Relax around the table
23. Gather round the table
24. Really solid tables for real families
25. Linger round the table
26. Elegant dining at home
27. Host the party

Introductory Statements

1. Beveled glass doors, to highlight your treasured china, heirlooms and collectibles.
2. A softly lighted cabinet to showcase your dinnerware and find china.
3. Finely crafted drawers, roomy and deep enough to store your linens and flatware.
4. Perfect - whether it's a candlelight dinner for two or holiday celebration for eight.
5. An informal grouping of tables and chairs in golden oak, to perfectly complement a sunny breakfast nook or kitchen.
6. Gather around for Monopoly, homework, pizza or cornflakes - this dinette is a versatile and attractive choice for years of use.
7. A glossy, hand-rubbed finish reflects your pride in your new dining room.
8. Not merely furnishings in your home…but a part of your family memories.
9. Grace in design. Strength in construction. Versatile in function.
10. Hand-carved backs mean you add a warm, country look to your kitchen or dining room.
11. Solidly-designed chairs reminiscent of Grandma's kitchen, where you always found the warmth of heart and home.
12. You'll enjoy American quality and craftsmanship with this solid ash table and chairs that are made to handle the wear and tear of your family's busy life. The table features an easy-care.
13. Formica top - which means it can take all the messes your kids can dish out and still come up looking great.
14. Contour-back chairs invite you to relax and enjoy the conversation over coffee even after you've finished dinner.
15. Your teenager pushes away from the table as he rushes off to band practice and your grade-schooler leans across to get the sugar bowl. Our double pedestal table is sturdy enough to take the bumps and knocks of real use by real families day in and day out.
16. Swivel-tilt arm chairs, which means you can pass the potatoes and keep your eye on the big game without getting a crick in your neck!
17. Genuine tile top, which means you have beauty, durability and a built-in hot plate all in one great table!
18. Table extends to 66', which means you can invite the boss, his wife and all their kids over for dinner.
19. Table extends to 66', which means you can invite even more friends to your next dinner party.
20. The beauty of a pedestal table - but built solidly enough to handle the bumps and jostles of family dinners night after night.

21. The simplicity of this Shaker style dining room set will help you savor a simple dinner with the family every night.
22. The solidly-built chairs around this table won't loosen or become unstable with the use your family dishes out.
23. This all-wood country dining room set is just what you need to make your room inviting and comfortable.
24. Need a dining room set that match the elegance of your formal dining room? This sophisticated set offers upscale design, fine detailing, intricate patterns and inlays - all beautifully woven together in a set that will become the focal point for fine dining.
25. The smooth lines and floral designs in this French country style dining set will bring the beauty and relaxation of the outdoors to your mealtimes.
26. The practical Formica" top on this table will make cleaning up spills a breeze.
27. The finer grain in our solid birch dining furniture brings a different look to your room, while giving you all the strength and durability of any solid wood.
28. The warmth and strength of this solid oak dining group will grace your dining room with beauty for many, many years.
29. The quality construction in this solid wood dining set will withstand years of use by your active family.
30. Practical, attractive and durable, this farmhouse dining set will bring a touch of country relaxation to your family's mealtime.
31. With a chopping block, wire basket storage and towel bar, this country-style island will make your kitchen more charming and your work easier!

RECLINERS

Headings

1. Have a seat
2. You deserve a special place of your own…a (brand name) recliner
3. Styled - and priced - for comfort
4. Choose a style. Choose a fabric. Choose a price
5. We've got more recliners than we can count
6. Lean back…relax…you've found the best selection of recliners in town
7. Had a hard day? Kick back in one of these great recliners. Feel the stress go away
8. Recliners - a better way to sit
9. Recliners take you back
10. Put your feet up - with one of your beautiful recliners
11. Great recliners. Great buys.
12. A relaxing thought - a new recliner at a terrific price
13. Sink into a recliner.
14. If you don't have a seat for the big game - get one
15. Give the best seat in the house to Dad! He deserves it
16. Give the best seat in the house to Mom! She deserves it

1. It's a comfortable spot at the end of the day…it's a way to leave the stress behind.
2. . . . It's a great addition to your room…it's a recliner.
3. You'd never guess it's a recliner!
4. Smooth controls mean no bumps or jolts when you settle back for a snooze or your favorite show.
5. Morning paper or afternoon nap - the style and ergonomic design of our recliners keep you comfortable any hour of the day.
6. Our new generation of recliners features stylish good looks, which means they fit your living room's elegant look without the traditional 'recliner' styling.
7. That's a recliner?
8. Features an expansive back, thickly-cushioned seat and flared padded arms - which means you'll have more than enough room and comfort when you settle down to watch your favorite show.
9. Plenty of room and lots of comfort await you with this expansive-backed and thickly-cushioned seat and padded arms.
10. You'll enjoy full-body comfort, which is just what you need to wind down from a rough day on the job.
11. Wind down from a tough work day with full-body comfort.
12. Generous padding in the arms and seat provide a great fit - which means great comfort when you're ready to kick back and relax.
13. Great fit and unbelievable comfort is what you get with these generously-padded arms and seat.
14. Has a triple back and a chaise set that reclines to one continuous surface - what a great way to leave the stress of the world behind!
15. Let the stress melt as you recline in this triple-backed, continuous-surface chaise set!
16. There's a built-in speaker phone and modem jack for easy laptop computer access – you've never had a more comfortable office!
17. Two soothing heat settings and six massage motors that work individually or together for a full body massage - like having a personal massage therapist on duty 24 hours a day in your own home!
18. Your own personal masseuse with two soothing heat settings and six massage motors to ease the stresses of your day.
19. Unwind after a long day and let the built-in massage in this great recliner help you relax.
20. With this swivel recliner, you can easily move to converse with another person or get a better view of the TV - and enjoy reclining comfort all the way.
21. Mobility and massage, all in one recliner!
22. Love a recliner but need one with more room? Here's the ticket. The generous scaling gives anyone plenty of room to relax and kick back.
23. Want a recliner with more room? Here's the ticket. The generous scaling gives anyone plenty of room to relax and kick back.

24. Love a recliner but have a small room? Here's the answer. You can place this comfortable recliner as close as three inches to the wall and still have room to kick back.
25. The contemporary styling in this living room group gives your room a modern yet comfortable look.
26. Thought you couldn't have the style you love with a recliner? Check out this high leg recliner with refined Chippendale styling and relax in high style.
27. A Chippendale recliner? You bet!
28. No one will ever know it's a recliner - until you tell them.
29. Incredible reclineables! Reclining furniture that looks great, too!

LIVING ROOMS

Headings

1. The most comfortable spot in the house
2. Sectional seating - room to live
3. Reading, cuddling, snoozing, lounging…just a few of the reasons you'll love our living rooms
4. Incredible reclineables! Reclining furniture that looks great, too
5. Choose the fabric, choose the price! Isn't this nice?
6. It's soft…it's durable…it's colorful…and yes, it's really leather
7. Leather for everyday living
8. Beautiful…functional…fabulous furniture for your living room
9. Save on sofas
10. Comfort sale. Special discounts on selected living rooms
11. Relax! All of our reclining furniture is on sale
12. Save now, snooze later
13. Get comfortable with up to 00% off of all living rooms
14. The weather might be frightful, but our Living Room Sale is delightful….come in
15. Living rooms you can really live in
16. The finest furniture for the finest living
17. Terrific living room furniture - at prices you can live with
18. Invite the neighborhood – there's room for all with these sectionals
19. Video night's even more fun with these versatile living rooms
20. Versatility, comfort and good looks meet in these living rooms
21. Choices and more choices in living rooms
22. Living rooms with style and comfort
23. Gather the family together in these great living rooms
24. Cozy living rooms - bringing people together
25. Kick back and enjoy the game
26. Sturdy construction, lasting beauty
27. Settle down in comfort
28. Beautifully coordinated living rooms
29. Tough construction for everyday use

30. Stain resistant, family friendly
31. Choose the perfect fabric, color
32. Put your feet up
33. Sectionals - last word in versatility
34. Easy on your back
35. Sink into comfort
36. Classic to modern, take your pick
37. Enjoy the richness of leather
38. You like to keep them guessing. Check out these sectionals.
39. You get bored easily. Sectionals keep the design possibilities open.

Introductory Statements

1. Stain-resistant treatments keep your upholstery looking beautiful year after year.
2. Durable, practical yet beautiful fabrics mean your new living room set is functional - yet with an appearance you can take pride in.
3. Beautiful and fully functional. The combination you've been looking for.
4. Messy spills and accidents? No problem with our stain-resistant fabrics designed to take all the punishment your family can dole out.
5. The velvety comfort of cushions and pillow-back styling and invite you to sit a spell . . . And stay a while.
6. Sink into the fragrance and suppleness of real leather. A timeless choice for a classic sofa.
7. This five-piece living room set includes a sofa, loveseat, cocktail table and two end tables, which means you can have a whole new, perfectly coordinated living room all at once!
8. Outfit your living room in one fell swoop with this five-piece sent featuring a sofa, loveseat, cocktail table and two end tables!
9. This is an updated look with nailheads, hand applied and trimming each wonderful curve, right down to the solid wood spindle leg - which means your home will enjoy a new air of elegance and sophistication.
10. Hand-applied nailheads add that touch of sophistication to each wonderful curve, including the solid wood spindle leg.
11. Hardwood frame, which means you'll have a sofa that's built to last.
12. If you want a sofa that's built to last, choose the one built on a hard-wood frame.
13. Pillows, which mean you can nestle down in comfort.
14. Sink into the softness of pillows, piled high and waiting for you!
15. Matching pillows and chairs, which means your entire room will be beautifully coordinated.
16. Coordinate and beautify your room at the same time with matching pillows and chairs.
17. Just in case your kids ever jump, flop or wrestle on the couch, this sofa has a tough coil spring seating that will still be comfortable when you sit on the couch.
18. Want your couch to be comfortable after the kids have had their way with it? Select one with a tough coil spring.

19. Stain-resistant material, which means you don't have to worry about the juice your son just spilled.
20. Forget about spills with this stain-resistant material.
21. Sturdy material that stands up to the wear and tear of three kids and dog on the sofa all at once.
22. You need sturdy fabric that stands up to a family's wear and tear.
23. Choice of fabric, which means you can get just the right color to match the blues in that terrific old painting you found at the auction.
24. You can match colors perfectly with our huge selection of fabric.
25. Fold-down tray with cup-holders, which means you can have all your snacks and drinks at your fingertips - without interrupting the mystery video to go get them!
26. Have your snacks and drinks at your fingertips with these cool fold-down trays with cup-holders!
27. Sectional with recliners, which means you've got seating that super-comfortable and super versatile.
28. Sectional and recliners in one? Talk about comfort and versatility in one package!
29. Sectional with recliners, which means you can put your feet up, even if your spouse and kids don't care to do the same.
30. Do your own thing! Feel like putting your feet up on the recliner but your hubby doesn't?
31. Doesn't matter with this sectional/recliner combination. You do, he doesn't. Life is good!
32. Supportive back, which means your tired back can get the rest it needs.
33. Give your tired, aching back the rest it needs with this supportive back.
34. You'll breathe a sigh of relief as you sink down into relaxing comfort of the generous cushions on this great sofa.
35. You'll breathe a sigh of relief as you sink down into relaxing comfort of the ultra padded seats on this great sofa.
36. Sink into the relaxing comfort of ultra padded sofa cushions.
37. Sink into the relaxing comfort of generous sofa cushions.
38. Give your living room or family room a truly classy look with the classic lines of this Chippendale sofa.
39. Capture timeless and classic design with this Chippendale sofa.
40. Your living room turns into a guest room when this terrific sofa turns into a comfortable bed, which means you're always ready to welcome friends and family.
41. Have double-duty rooms? Welcome friends and family a truly comfortable night's rest with this sofa bed.
42. Elegant design, giving you the perfect centerpiece for your room's decor.
43. Leather, which means you'll enjoy the rich look and feel that only genuine leather can give.
44. Sit back and enjoy the rich look and feel that only leather can give.
45. With channel-stitched tailoring that creates softly pillowed bustlebacks, you'll sink into this sofa with a sigh of contentment.
46. Channel-stitching creates that soft, pillowed look that you love to sink into.
47. Channel-stitching creates that soft, pillowed look that invites you to sink into.

48. It's a softly pillowed sofa and a recliner - a great place to snuggle with the kids while you read them a book.
49. Snuggle with a loved one, or two, with this softly-pillowed sofa-recliner.
50. Wood accents bring a touch of elegance to this casual sofa, making it perfect for formal or informal rooms.
51. Wood accents create a touch of casual elegance, perfect for formal or informal design.
52. A traditional camel back sofa is comfortable and classy - and can both complement other.
53. Traditional pieces or contrast with modern furniture for an eclectic look.
54. Camel back sofas bridge the design gap between traditional and modern with classic elegance.
55. Camel back sofas marry traditional and modern design with classic elegance.
56. Like a modern look? This sofa has the clean lines of a great contemporary style plus the comfort of a deep pillow back.
57. Take comfort in this modern contemporary sofa featuring a deep pillow back.
58. Nothing's more practical than a slipcover sofa! Protect the fabric underneath from everyday wear and take the cover off completely for easy cleaning.
59. Create easy new looks and protect your sofa from wear and tear with slipcovers!
60. A classic design element, slipcovers can create drama, add elegance or bring in a casual air to your sofa.
61. You might start out wanting a slipcover to protect your sofa, but you'll end up buying several to change the mood or season of your living room!
62. Add interest to your room with an L-shaped reclining sectional - then kick-back and relax!
63. Leather. Nothing makes a stronger statement of elegance and comfort. Enjoy the beauty and durability of this classic leather style with nailhead trim.
64. The recliners, cockpit wedges and unparalleled comfort of this sectional will let you enjoy night after night with the whole family.
65. You don't have to get up when the phone rings with this sectional - cockpit wedges offer storage, a cordless phone and lumbar heated massage.
66. Here's the perfect focal point for your country style room - charming, comfortable and practical.
67. Reversible seat cushions mean your investment in this sofa will last twice as long!
68. The classic lines of this colonial-look sofa blend with both formal and informal styles - which means it will look great with all your furniture!
69. You'll love the button tufted style of this sofa, since it gives you a great look and extra comfort at the same time.
70. Wood accents, full pleated skirt, accent pillows - all the little extras on this classic sofa will bring'an extra touch of class to your home.
71. This popular sofa comes in so many colors because it looks great in so many - which means you can just choose the one that perfectly fits your decor.
72. This sofa is so comfortable and inviting, your family will want to relax together on it at the end of a busy day.
73. Such a deal! A charming country sofa that's easy to relax in and easy on your wallet!

BEDDING/MATTRESSES

Headings

1. Save big today…sleep well tonight
2. You won't find a better mattress at a better price. We guarantee it!
3. Get a really good night's rest - every night
4. You'll sleep tight on a mattress from Store Name
5. Wake up refreshed
6. Sturdy support and luxurious comfort combined in an affordable mattress
7. The princess would have never felt the pea with this mattress
8. Quality construction, quality materials, quality sleep
9. Put your worries to rest with our mattress
10. Sweet dreams
11. Mattresses made well so you'll sleep well
12. A great mattress = a great night's rest

Introductory Statements

1. The newest technologies in sleep comfort mean you get a healthful night's rest, a refreshing 'good morning.'
2. Get better Zzzzzzz's with A-plus design and comfort technology.
3. Pillow-cushioned comfort, designed to support every curve of your body.
4. Don' t snooze and lose - you win with a new mattress and box spring.
5. An investment in one-third of your life…the eight hours a day you (should) spend in bed.
6. Time to settle in for a long winter's nap on a (brand name) mattress set!
7. Plush top, which means you'll have all the comfort of a feather bed.
8. Sleep soundly in all the comfort of a feather bed with a plush top.
9. Can it hold eight kids, four hound dogs and a piggy you stole from the shed? If it can, it's either Grandma's feather bed or our durable _____ with sturdy coil springs.
10. The _____ foundation is strong enough to take the wear and tear your kids will give it and still give them a good night's rest.
11. Endorsed and recommended by the American Chiropractic Association, which means this mattress is an investment in your good health.
12. Invest in your health! This mattress was endorsed and recommended by the American Chiropractic Association.
13. Endorsed by… , which means your back will thank you for a good night's rest.
14. Endorsed by…, which means you'll be treating your back right with this mattress.
15. Support, which means you can really rest tonight.
16. Support, which means you won't wake up with a stiff back or a crick in your neck - just with the energy to get your day off to a great start!
17. Start your day off right! Stiff backs and necks are a thing of the past when you sleep on (mention product).

18. Comfort, which means you can really enjoy a good night's rest.
19. You'll relax from head to toe as you drift off in the comfort this plush mattress gives.
20. Ahhhhh, comfort. Need we say more?

BEDROOMS

Headings

1. Welcome to your new private retreat
2. Bedrooms fit for a king - at prices you can afford
3. Wake up to class and comfort with one of these great bedroom suites
4. Unwind in comfort with our best bedroom furnishings. The finest bedroom furniture you'll find
5. Bedroom suites suited to your needs
6. Surround yourself with relaxation
7. Beautiful bedrooms for every budget
8. Sweet dreams await you in your new bedroom
9. Wake up refreshed
10. Your place to unwind
11. Enjoy your private retreat
12. Beautiful bedrooms
13. Wake up in a beautiful room

Introductory Statements

1. The solid wood design and fine craftsmanship means you're looking at tomorrow's fine antiques - today.
2. Create tomorrow's antiques today by selecting solid wood design and fine craftsmanship.
3. Your hideaway from the hassles and hurries of your harried lifestyle.
4. Nestle into your new four poster bed, and savor your new bedroom retreat.
5. What's more romantic than a four poster bed?
6. Amish-inspired, carved headboards and accents mean a combination of timeless tradition with simple beauty.
7. Timeless tradition and simple beauty abound in this collection of Amish-inspired, carved headboards and accents.
8. Cedar-lined drawers, which means your clothes will smell fresh and clean.
9. Be kind to your clothes with cedar-lined drawers.
10. Hand carvings, which mean your bedroom will have a distinctive, elegant look.
11. Enjoy the distinctive, elegant look of hand carved wood.
12. Ball bearing drawer glides bear more weight, which means you can store more in your drawer!
13. Don't be timid about stuffing dresser drawers. Ball bearing drawer glides bear more weight with ease.

19

14. Ball bearing drawer glides last longer, which means your beautiful new bedroom suites may well become the next family heirloom.
15. Keep your furniture for future generations. Ball bearing drawer glides add long life to your furniture.
16. Ball bearing drawer glides roll easier, which means you won't have to fight a stuck dresser drawer when you're rushing to get out the door to work.
17. Don't fight with your dresser drawers! This (mention piece) is fitted with ball bearing drawer glides for ease in use.
18. Solid oak, which means you'll have beautiful furniture strong enough to live with, not just look at.
19. Solid oak furniture is not for the timid – it's for people who use their furniture, not just look at it.
20. Coordinated pieces, which mean you can completely furnish your bedroom in a brand new, great look.
21. Not a designer? Not to worry. Coordinated pieces take the guesswork out of design.
22. Simplify your life! The clean lines of this Mission and Shaker styling combination will help bring order and relaxation to your bedroom's look.
23. What spells simplicity better than the timeless design traditions of Shaker and Mission? Bring a little ordered elegance into your life.
24. Bring a unique look to your bedroom with this sleigh bed. Let it bring a touch of yesteryear to your room that will help you relax and wake more refreshed.
25. Sweeping romantic lines in this sleighbed usher you into dreams of yesteryear.
26. Lose yourself in the timeless elegance of this romantic sleighbed.

YOUTH BEDDING/GROUPS

Headings

1. Designs that will grow with your child
2. Fun bedrooms for kids
3. Kid-friendly furniture
4. A bedroom your kid will love
5. Sturdy for play, comfort

Introductory Statements

1. From tot to teenager, these convertible designs change to meet the needs of your child.
2. From tot to teen - convertible bedrooms that grow with your child.
3. Every little girl's dream…a canopy bed of her very own.
4. Your daughter's a little princess…a canopy bed of her very own.
5. No odds or ends or grown-up furniture to fit into - your daughter deserves a bedroom of fairy tales come true.
6. Make your daughter's dreams come true.

7. Odds-and-ends furniture doesn't last a lifetime. This (mention product) will.
8. Rugged, rough and tumble…bedroom furniture for boys. Tough, yet handsome enough to leave the bedroom door open wide with pride.
9. Bunk beds are sturdy, which means your kids can turn them into tepees, space ships or caves – they'll turn back into comfortable beds when the kids turn in.
10. Sturdy bunk beds are really tepees, space ships and caves in disguise. Didn't you know that?
11. Kid-friendly, which means your kids will love the cubby-holes, hidden storage areas and nested bunks that will make their bedroom an adventure room.
12. Turn your kids' room into an adventure room! Cubbies, hidden storage and nested bunks are a natural!
13. Heat catalyzed varnish, which means the dresser will be okay even if your daughter spills her fingernail polish on it.
14. Spilled nail polish on the dresser? Not to worry with heat catalyzed varnish.
15. Your kids will love this fun style of pine furniture; you'll love the durability of the solid wood.
16. Fun-styled furniture for your kids - solid pine furniture for you.
17. Okay, you've told the kids not to jump on the bed. Don't tell them that this one can take it.
18. The frame is engineered with eleven points of support for great strength.
19. Don't tell the kids they really can jump on the bed even though they really can. With eleven points of support, this bed is engineered for superior strength.
20. It's not just a bedroom, it's a playroom! Your kids will love the upper bed, the cubbyholes and the fun that this bunk bed set offers.
21. Ask any kid what kind of bed he wants - the answer is always the same: a bunk bed of course!
22. What kid wouldn't want this bunk bed, turning bedtime into playtime!

ENTERTAINMENT CENTERS

Headings

1. A place for everything
2. Relax and enjoy
3. Flexible, beautiful, convenient
4. Everything you need for entertainment
5. Entertainment centers you can really enjoy
6. Entertainment centers you'll love
7. Enjoy perfect views, perfect sounds
8. End clutter and beautify
9. Beautifully simple

1. Not just a convenient place for your television or stereo, but a stylish complement to your decor.
2. Don't let them see the cords and plugs - just the beauty.
3. A showcase for your state-of-the-art electronic equipment, at the same time, a handsome addition to your surroundings.
4. Showcase your state-of-the-art electronic equipment - beautifully!
5. Showcase your state-of-the-art electronic equipment - handsomely!
6. Casters, which mean you can easily rearrange your room without breaking your back!
7. Don't break your back moving furniture! One word: casters!
8. Glass doors, which means you can display your favorite collection and keep it dust-free.
9. Don't dust! (Mention product) features glass doors to show off your collections!
10. Holds _____ TV, which means you'll have a great view of all your favorite shows.
11. Adjustable shelves, which mean you can store everything - small or tall!
12. Your life is full of change - adjust to it with adjustable shelves!
13. Ample storage space, which means you'll finally have a great place to keep all those videos that seem to clutter the room.
14. Too many videos you can't part with? Store them in (mention product), thoughtfully designed with ample storage space.
15. Corner piece, which means you'll make great use of every inch of space in your room.
16. Corner pieces - masterpieces of design space and style!
17. Pocket doors – won't it be great to have the doors just disappear so they don't block anyone's view or get bumped by people walking by?
18. Pocket doors tuck away for ease in viewing.
19. Swivel top (for entertainment stands), so you can enjoy the perfect view.
20. Catch every angle with a swivel top entertainment stand.
21. Customize your entertainment center to fit your screen, your storage needs, your style. And enjoy night after night of great entertainment!
22. This entertainment center can handle all your needs for storage and hook-ups - and then close up to double as a beautiful piece of furniture!
23. The best of both worlds - elegant design, ergonomic storage.

HOME OFFICE

Headings

1. Streamlined and efficient . . . both you and your surroundings
2. Home office furniture that fits your business and lifestyle
3. Furniture that works as hard as you do . . . in the comfort of your home
4. Organize your home office with these great pieces

5. Affordable office furniture for your growing business
6. There's a place for everything with our specially-designed home office furniture
7. Work efficiently, work comfortably
8. More than desks and chairs - we have complete home office furnishings
9. Tough enough for the kids, stylish and useful enough for you - great home office furniture
10. You work at home, you live at home. Do both better with our home office furnishings.
11. The bottom line is savings in home office furniture
12. Organize your life
13. A place for everything
14. Yesterday's look, today's technology
15. Storage with style
16. A home office uniquely yours
17. Efficiency with the warmth of home

Introductory Statements

1. Generous doors and drawers help you tuck away the clutter of a busy day.
2. It's all about image. Professional and organized – that's what our office groupings say to your customers.
3. Plenty of room for computer, which means you can handle the smallest laptop or the biggest tower.
4. Specialized storage areas, which mean you'll be more organized and efficient than ever before, from CDs to reference books.
5. From CDs to reference books, specialized storage areas keep you organized.
6. Rolltop desk, which means you'll have the look and style of yesterday, with customized features for tomorrow's technology.
7. Delight in the warm look of yesteryear surrounded by customized high-tech features.
8. Pigeon holes, which mean you won't get the grocery list mixed up with the bills or tomorrows mail.
9. Convenient pigeon holes organize your hectic life.
10. Locking file drawers, which means your kids won't be able to use your tax records for drawing paper.
11. Safe and secure with locking file drawers.
12. Large storage areas, which mean you can take advantage of that sale on copy paper!
13. Desk with hutch, which means you can keep important things within reach but out of the way.
14. Keep important items within easy reach but off the desk surface with convenient hutch. Legal-sized drawers, giving you more room, more versatility.
15. Pull-out writing surfaces, which means extra usable space and extra convenience.
16. Need extra surface area but don't have the floor space? Pull-out writing surfaces save the day!

17. All sizes of bookcases - and there's one to fit you, whether you're a casual reader or a serious bookworm.
18. Bookcases aren't just for books!
19. Lawyer's bookcase, which means you can read your books without dusting them first!
20. Keeps dust off your book collection with lawyer's bookcases featuring glass doors for style and convenience.
21. Pull-out tray for keyboard, which means you'll have more room on the desk and less chance of strain on your arms and back!
22. Well-designed pull-out keyboard tray reduces strain on your back.
23. Pull-out shelf for printer, which means it's there when you need it, and hidden when you don't.
24. Pull-out printer shelf is there when you need it, and hidden when you don't.
25. Modern conveniences and storage areas combined with this beautiful traditional style mean that you'll enjoy a modern home office without compromising the comfortable look of your home.
26. Don't compromise the beauty of your home! (Mention product) combines modern
27. Conveniences and traditional styling in one, gorgeous home office.
28. This computer workstation has a place for everything, which means it will be easier for you to keep everything in its place!
29. Keep everything in its place with this computer workstation.
30. The classic beauty of a rolltop desk with modern conveniences of a computer workstation are combined in this computer roll top - which means technology and traditional beauty are both at your fingertips.
31. Ingenious design combines classic rolltop features with modern computer workstation elements.

RUGS/CARPETING/FLOORING

Headings

1. Kid-proof flooring
2. Beautiful, comfortable floors
3. Stain resistant, beauty irresistible
4. Hundreds of colors - pick your favorite
5. Floors that say elegance

Introductory Statements

1. Nubby neutrals of our popular Berbers fit any need, from casual to elegant.
2. The deep, rich jewel-like tones of our Orientals bring an exquisite depth to your room setting.
3. Surround yourself in wall-to-wall softness and luxury with our finest line of carpeting.

4. Wriggle your toes into the deep piles and soft colors of our quality wall-to-wall carpet.
5. Arrange your chair, sofa or loveseat around a designer border rug and create a cozy conversational grouping…or an elegant sitting area.
6. Oriental area rugs ground your floor plan with elegance and distinction
7. Top your polished hardwood floors with an oasis of plush comfort - choose from a rainbow of hues in stain-resistant area rugs.
8. The beauty of wood flooring without the fuss. Explore the affordable option of hardwood-look laminates.
9. Kid-proof, which means it can take spilled milk, muddy shoes and puppy accidents - and come up clean with just a damp cloth.
10. Thicker, which means you have more cushioning for your tired feet at the end of the day.
11. Formica¨ flooring resists impacts, which means that if you toddler knocks over the flower pot, you just have to worry about the flower, not the flooring.
12. Formica¨ flooring resists stains, which means you can relax during dinner - even with preschoolers at the table.
13. Relax, Formica flooring resists stains
14. Relax, Formica flooring resists impact damage.
15. Subtle blend of diverse colors, which means you can change the look of the room without changing the carpet.
16. Using a subtle blend of many colors allows you to change the look of your rooms without changing the carpet.
17. Great selection of colors, which means you're sure to find just the right one to tie your whole look together.
18. Static-free - this beautiful rug will impress your guests, but not shock them!

OUTDOOR FURNITURE

Headings

1. Tough but comfortable
2. Bring the indoors out
3. Serene garden time

Introductory Statements

1. Your outdoor 'living' room - complete with functional furnishings as comfortable as the ones inside your home.
2. Bring the comfort of inside living outdoors.
3. Cushiony and comfortable with styles that will keep their color and good looks year after year.
4. Poolside or garden setting…this line of outdoor furnishing will help you enjoy the good life -in your own backyard.

5. Tough, coated finishes are durable and beautiful, withstanding rain, sun, heat and frost.
6. Comfortable but tough, which means you can relax with your lemonade this afternoon and not worry about a little rain tonight.

ACCESSORIES/MISCELLANEOUS

Headings

1. Neat ideas
2. Neat ideas for your home
3. Little things that make a big difference
4. Enlightening ideas! (for lighting)
5. Save on the finishing touches
6. Furnishing values you can be comfortable with
7. We have what you want
8. We have the look you want
9. Popular looks at popular prices
10. Values for every home and budget
11. Furnishing for every home and budget
12. Gifts to add the perfect finishing touch to your room.
13. A beautiful gift today…a treasured keepsake tomorrow
14. Finishing touches you'll love
15. Tie your home together with these tasteful accessories
16. The lap for your corner table, the hat rack for your hall…we've got all the accessories your home needs
17. Ready for finishing touches? You've come to the right place
18. Accessorize your entire home
19. Make your home truly yours with accessories
20. Endless choices in accessories
21. Just the right touch for every room
22. Your style, your tastes - we have just the right accessories for you
23. Pick your favorites – we've got what you need to complete your look
24. The right look, the right prices
25. It's the little things that make a room
26. Crystal…fine porcelain…sculpture and glass. Our fine accessories provide the finishing touch to any room
27. Make your house a home, with the crowing touch of a fine accessory piece for your mantel or table
28. The crowning touches
29. The finishing touches
30. Accent your room in style
31. Accent your home in style
32. The perfect accents
33. Just what you've wanted

34. Little things make a big difference
35. Your own finishing touches
36. Mood lighting - of course

Introductory Statements

1. Bring a touch of international flavor to your home with this hand-decorated bombe secretary - and enjoy a conversational piece that's as practical as it is unique.
2. Make a statement with this hand-decorated bombe secretary.
3. They're not just for books. Use these beautiful bookcases as a focal point in your room or to display your favorite things.
4. This armoire will stand the test of time and use. Its sturdy construction will give you years of use while its classic design enhances the beauty of your home.
5. Cast a golden glow of welcome with a graceful brass floor lamp.
6. Make a small room bigger with light! Try these beautiful floor or table lamps.
7. Mirrors - a reflection of the beautiful home you're created for your family.
8. Double the room's size with mirrors!
9. Reflect the beauty of your home with mirrors!
10. Have a small room? A mirror will make it look bigger. Try this class design.
11. You won't need a 'mirror, mirror on the wall' with this cheval style floor mirror - and its rich oak beauty will make your room the fairest one of all.
12. Cheval mirrors add grace and nostalgia to your room.
13. Chain-driven Westminster chimes, which mean beautiful sounds will echo through your home as the clock marks the time.
14. Let beautiful sounds echo through your home with chain-driven Westminster chimes.
15. Mark time beautifully with chain-driven Westminster chimes.
16. Elongated glass door, which means your clock adds beauty and interest to your home.
17. Silent option, for those days when you feel like stopping the march of time.
18. Chimes drive you nuts? Then silent option is for you.
19. Grandfather clocks are all-time favorites! Use this one as a beautiful focal point in any room in your home.
20. Mark the passage of the day with the stately chimes of our Westminster clocks.
21. An upholstered chair and rocking chair in one piece, which means you may get comfortable enough to go to sleep yourself while you rock the baby.
22. This glide rocker will add a homespun look to your decor.
23. A traditional or welcome gift for graduation or engagement - any young woman would treasure a cedar chest.
24. Tasteful design, spacious storage and aromatic cedar, which means you'll have beauty,
25. Usefulness and fresh-smelling clothes all wrapped up in the great tradition of a cedar chest.

26. Corner design means more of your favorite collection can be seen, while taking up less space in the room. Halogen lighting, which will bring out the best in your best pieces.
27. Adjustable shelves, which mean you can customize this great cupboard to fit your special items.
28. Adjust the shelves to showcase your special items.
29. Adjust the shelves to highlight your favorite things.
30. Mirrored back, which means your pieces will look doubly lovely!
31. Mirrored back shows off every inch of your treasures.
32. This curio cabinet gives you lots of extra room for that special collection while keeping it dust-free and in full view for you and your guests to enjoy.
33. Power lift. Even if you have trouble getting in and out of a regular recliner, you can enjoy putting your feet up with this power lift recliner.
34. Side pocket, which means you can keep your favorite book or magazine hand.
35. It's the little things that matter, like this side pocket for handy storage.
36. A table that's more than a table! This cocktail table offers storage, hinged side pieces and the practicality of a glass top with the beauty of wood construction.
37. Oak solid with glass top gives you solid construction with the open look of glass.
38. Opposites attract in this solid oak table with glass insert.

STYLES

1. Contemporary - as sleek and up-to-date as your outlook on life.
2. Victorian - celebrating craftsmanship and design of a bygone era.
3. Country - taking pride in the finely-honed simplicity of our American heritage.
4. Mission - hearkens to a time of nature and the earth's bounty
5. Southwestern - the warmth and simple lines of the American southwest.
6. Queen Anne - the warm, rich luster of cherry adds elegance beyond measure.
7. Windsor styling - a tradition of classic simplicity

SEASONAL

1. Beat the winter blahs
2. Cure for cabin fever
3. This price will get your blood going
4. This price will get your temperature rising
5. Our prescription for beating the winter blues
6. Sweetheart savings.
7. A sale to fall in love with
8. 'Spring' time - bounce in for savings
9. April shower of savings
10. Easter hunt for savings
11. blooming bargains
12. Carefree summer style

13. Sail into summer
14. Summer breezes blow warm
15. It's summertime and the saving is easy
16. Firecracker savings
17. Rodeo round up
18. Dog days sale...dog gone good deals
19. Back to math class...go figure the savings
20. Falling leaves, falling prices
21. Autumn haven
22. '50's Cruise, hot rod savings
23. Holiday open house
24. Winter woes into winter Oooohs

TRENDY, PERSONAL EXPRESSIONS

1. Express your style
2. Family and comfort first
3. Embrace your space
4. Create the home you've always wanted
5. Great style!
6. Create romance
7. Add romance
8. Suit the season
9. Reinvent your space
10. Home and hearth
11. Welcome home
12. Rejuvenate your living space
13. Here's how to get the look you love
14. Fresh & new
15. Comfort zone
16. Everything you need to make your house a home
17. Create a welcome space
18. Relax and renew
19. Enduring elegance
20. Identify your own space
21. Make it your home
22. Make tour home your place
23. Elegance and simplicity
24. Elegant simplicity
25. Pare down, simplify your space (closets, living areas, etc.)
26. Create your own retreat
27. Express yourself!
28. Create your own workspace at home
29. Your home is your refuge
30. Your space is just that - yours! Take charge of it!

31. Create a kid-friendly home.
32. Don't forget the kids
33. Relax and renew in your own retreat
34. Come home
35. Make your home a welcome place
36. Draw your family together
37. Bring the family home
38. Comfort is key to a welcoming home
39. Style brings out your personality
40. Relax in the comfort of your home space
41. A quiet niche needs comfortable furniture
42. A quiet niche calls for comfortable furniture
43. The elements of style are within your grasp
44. The elements of style are yours
45. Bring out your personality with style
46. Fill your home with comfort and style
47. Personalize your space
48. Personalize your home
49. Personalize your home office

SAVVY, SASSY, SOPHISTICATED

Fill-In-The-Blanks and Starters

1. Easy to impress
2. Aim your quest for the newest, smartest, coolest.
3. Direct your quest for the newest, smartest, coolest.
4. Go for the sassy.
5. Intelligent and oh, so good looking!
6. Vibrant, versatile and vulnerable . . .
7. For the first time
8. Welcome him home - in style
9. Welcome him back - in style
10. It has arrived
11. You aren't a child - go for it
12. Ergonomically designed to comfort and support your body, not fight it
13. Precision adjustable components give you a comfortable, natural fit
14. When it feels as good as it looks
15. Mmmm. Feels good
16. Make a great first impression
17. You can't go wrong
18. Distinguished is good
19. Naughty and nice
20. Capture the mood
21. You can capture

22. Impress the hell out of your friends (Mention product)
23. Let them eat cake . . . you've got the (mention product)
24. Work smarter and achieve more goals with this (mention home office product)
25. Pull ahead of the pack with (mention home office product)
26. Cool, huh
27. Cultivate his style
28. Don't go crazy when rearranging the entertainment center
29. A little romance
30. He can tell you, it's in the details
31. He can tell you, handsome is cool, to.
32. Smart design takes the trauma out of decorating
33. Shock value
34. Shock wave
35. Shock 'em
36. It's your lifestyle, do something
37. Go ahead and do it
38. As graceful as it is strong (well-built, sturdy)
39. Exquisite detail
40. Precise attention to detail
41. Give him some gee-whiz pleasure
42. All the rage
43. Sharing interests can be rewarding to both of you - include him in the decorating.
44. He knows how to fly under the radar
45. Conquer rough office terrain with this exquisite (home office product, desk, file cabinet, etc.)
46. Navigate through rivers of electronic equipment with
47. Navigate through rough waters to organize your
48. Encourage him to spend time at home
49. Launch the holidays with the purchase of
50. Rich selection
51. Not too flashy and not too dull
52. Ours exclusively
53. Brighten up the den or workroom with
54. Getting older has its advantages, like this heirloom quality
55. In a word, wow
56. You can access your favorite
57. . . . denotes the full measure of character inherent in today's
58. One of the great things about this
59. Favorite friends remind us that...should be about having fun
60. Inspired by
61. These elegantly understated
62. Crafted in . . . leather
63. A dream team for (mention category, i.e. home office, bedroom, etc.)
64. He's always dreamed of
65. You've always dreamed of
66. She's always dreamed of

67. Finally, a
68. Help him shake things up at home
69. Raise the bar in your (mention category)
70. From the masters of design
71. It's almost like having your own personal butler
72. Wake up in the best of this distinctive
73. Flashback to the '40s with
74. The retro style makes for
75. Bridge the technology gap with
76. For the ultimate
77. The future is here
78. The future is here and it's amazing
79. Expand your repertoire with
80. Intended to impress
81. Never have an extra chair handy?
82. Ingeniously integrated
83. We're not sure which is cooler about these
84. He can enjoy his favorite music or television show without
85. Handcrafted
86. Handy is an understatement here
87. Classic is an understatement here
88. High-powered performance
89. Your treasure hunt begins with
90. It's all in the attention to details
91. Magic moments
92. We strive to bring you the best collection of
93. Another year draws to a close
94. You're in the mood for a change
95. Regal airs
96. Elevated expectations
97. Surround yourself with fine accessories that capture your feminine sense of style
98. Great gift item
99. The lacquered finish helps protect the elegant surface from scratches. Catch all the colors of the rainbow
100. Serenity, simplicity, sophistication
101. Experience the calming effects of
102. Balance your hectic lifestyle with the simple, clean design of
103. Night magic
104. Tabletop tranquility
105. A Zen Garden
106. Encourage the flow of positive energy in your home (office) with the
107. Inner calm
108. Essence of color
109. It's a wrap
110. From the heart
111. Get the point

112. The perfect touch
113. Sense appeal
114. Calming influences
115. Twice as nice
116. Color spots
117. Organized fashion
118. Desktop divinity
119. Mountain masterpiece
120. Shelf stretchers
121. Picks for professionals
122. Ponderosa perfect (leather furniture)
123. Cleverly concealed
124. Let all the clutter disappear behind the closed doors of this . . .
125. One of the finest names in design . . .
126. Sleek silhouettes
127. Anything but boring
128. Classic appeal
129. The distinctly feminine styling of this
130. Ladylike leather
131. Slim and trim
132. Pointed presentations
133. Hooked on classics
134. Technology tamer
135. Full color confidence
136. Career casual
137. Polished fashion
138. Secret agent style
139. Got a minute?
140. Vintage collection
141. Illuminated curves
142. Artfully woven
143. Uplift your office
144. Check it out
145. Happy hues
146. Fresh outlook
147. Polished image
148. Pillow soft
149. Be kind to your shoulder (back)
150. Expert witness
151. Double the fun
152. Just like home
153. Really ripped
154. Metal miracles
155. Be bold and beautiful
156. Laptop luxury
157. Modern edges

158. Animal magnetism
159. Luxury in leather
160. Defining moments
161. Feed your phobia
162. Modern brilliance
163. Supine support
164. Focus on curves
165. Try one on
166. An evening in
167. Mirror In motion
168. City trekker
169. A case for keyboards
170. Not lost in space
171. So much stuff
172. Positive attitude
173. Disappearing act
174. Melt down your office
175. Something old, something new
176. Plane and solid geometry
177. New age style
178. Urban walker
179. Seasonal color
180. Space case
181. Fashion forward
182. Rearview raves
183. High style
184. Geometric genius
185. Art gallery chic
186. Asian influences
187. Piping hot style
188. Back to the future
189. Expect more from your . . .
190. Well connected
191. Unforgettable first impressions
192. Soft style
193. Tough duty
194. Trendy threads
195. Life in balance
196. Balancing…and
197. Fit for a Queen
198. Perfect pleasures
199. With love, from
200. Yes, Virginia, there is a Santa Claus
201. Eye-catching

Willie has chunks of deep smarts. He uniquely mixes 22 years of criminal justice experience with 28 years of marketing practice. He is most noted as being a marketing strategist, and has taught numerous seminars on that topic. He specializes in education-based marketing, and is a skilled copywriter who has written and developed successful, radio, TV, direct mail, and print advertising campaigns. He has previously authored three books. He is currently a managing member in Right Time, a faith-based start-up company committed to the prosocial reintegration of criminal offenders.

He may be contacted at...
willied@neo.rr.com